RESEARCH MISSION TO EARTH

RESEARCH MISSION TO EARTH

Simon Yeend
Daniel Limon

Collins

Contents

Chapter 1 Destination Earth 6

BONUS Amazing Earth 22

Chapter 2 Earthlings! 24

BONUS Earthlings: a guide for aliens 38

Chapter 3 Walking on the Moon 40

BONUS Earth and the Moon 54

Chapter 4 Life on Mars 56

BONUS How far away is the Moon? 70

Chapter 5 Danger! 72

BONUS The asteroid belt 86

Chapter 6 A race against time 88

BONUS Time on Earth 104

About the author 106

About the illustrator 108

Book chat 110

CHAPTER 1
Destination Earth

Audio Recording No. 1

Is this thing on?

Testing? Testing!

The light is blinking. I think it's working.

Right.

This is Zax checking in. Today I depart on my first solo mission to the Milky Way galaxy.

My destination? The small planet known as Earth and its moon.

As school projects go, this is quite a cool one. I get to travel to a distant galaxy, and I have to bring back rocks for the school rockery. All the rocks on Glibberon are perfectly round, and boring colours like pink, yellow and purple. Earth rocks come in all shapes and sizes, and moon rocks apparently are a super-cool light grey colour. They'll add some variety to the school rockery!

While I'm on Earth, I'd like to bring back a gift for Grandpa. He visited Earth in the time of Zorbon … wait … let me look it up in Earth years … in 1981. I bet it's changed. I'm going to surprise him.

Earth is straight on past Jupiter and then first right after Mars. Can't miss it.

This will be the furthest I have ever been from home. But it'll take me only a short time to get there, thanks to my Glibberon Glider, powered by a special energy source called Cosmic Crystals. The crystals bend space and time, so I can travel faster than light! I should be home in time for supper.

Completing final checklist.

Cosmic Crystals level. Full. Need enough to get there AND back! Check.

Earthling Camouflage Suit – I need to blend in. It used to belong to Grandpa, and he says it works fine … mostly. Check.

Earthling Manual. 1981 edition. Check.

Camera. Everyone will want to see my photos. Check.

Stellar, the on-board smart speaker. Working. Check.

And … what's this that Mum has scribbled on my list …? Toothbrush. Oh, Mum, good one! Check.

OK.

Earth time 15.00.

Time to blast off! Wish me luck!

End of transmission.

The journey gives me time to do my homework and discover some facts about this place called Earth. Here are five facts.

1 Earth is not a perfectly round ball – it's slightly squished! It's a bit flattened at the top and the bottom (the poles) and bulges around the middle (the equator).

2 Earth is the third closest planet to the Sun in this solar system. Mercury is the closest, then Venus.

3 Earth's position is in the 'Goldilocks Zone' – it's not too hot and not too cold. Earth's just far enough away from the Sun for water to remain liquid. If it was as far away as Saturn, the oceans would be frozen solid. If it was as close to the Sun as Mercury, the water would be boiling!

4 As well as water, Earth has the other essential thing that living creatures need to survive – oxygen.

5 Earth is the only planet in this solar system to have just one moon.

Audio Recording No. 2

Earth time 15.12

I've arrived. Five billion kilometres! My Earthling Manual tells me it would take their rockets 20 Earth years to travel that far. My Glibberon Glider made it in 12 Earth minutes. Which was quite slow, as I had to put on the brakes to dodge some space debris near Jupiter.

Hmmm. Earth is different to what I was expecting.

It looks like a large blueberry from up here. With green fungus spreading over it. Do Earthlings know their planet is going mouldy?

"Stellar, what are these white fluffy things in their atmosphere?"

"One moment, please ... Searching – "

Stellar takes a little time to warm up. My spaceship is a version 5. So old! But it's the only one my parents could afford and I love it.

"Zax, the white things are clouds."

Hmmm, they look tasty.

"Stellar, send reminder to Memory Log to eat a cloud – or several, if tasty – after landing."

But first I'm going on a tour of this interesting planet.

End of transmission.

That is a LOT of water. Stellar, what is the name of this huge puddle?

This is called the Pacific Ocean, the largest ocean on Earth.

Aah, I saw this from space. Stellar, what is it?

That is the Great Barrier Reef, near Australia. It's Earth's largest living structure, made mostly of coral reefs.

Stellar, why has Earth gone white and lumpy?

This is the highest point on the planet, and it is covered in snow. It is Earth's tallest mountain above sea level, Mount Everest.

Stellar, why is everything orange?

This is the Sahara Desert. There is little rainfall here, so there are few plants or animals, but LOTS of orange sand.

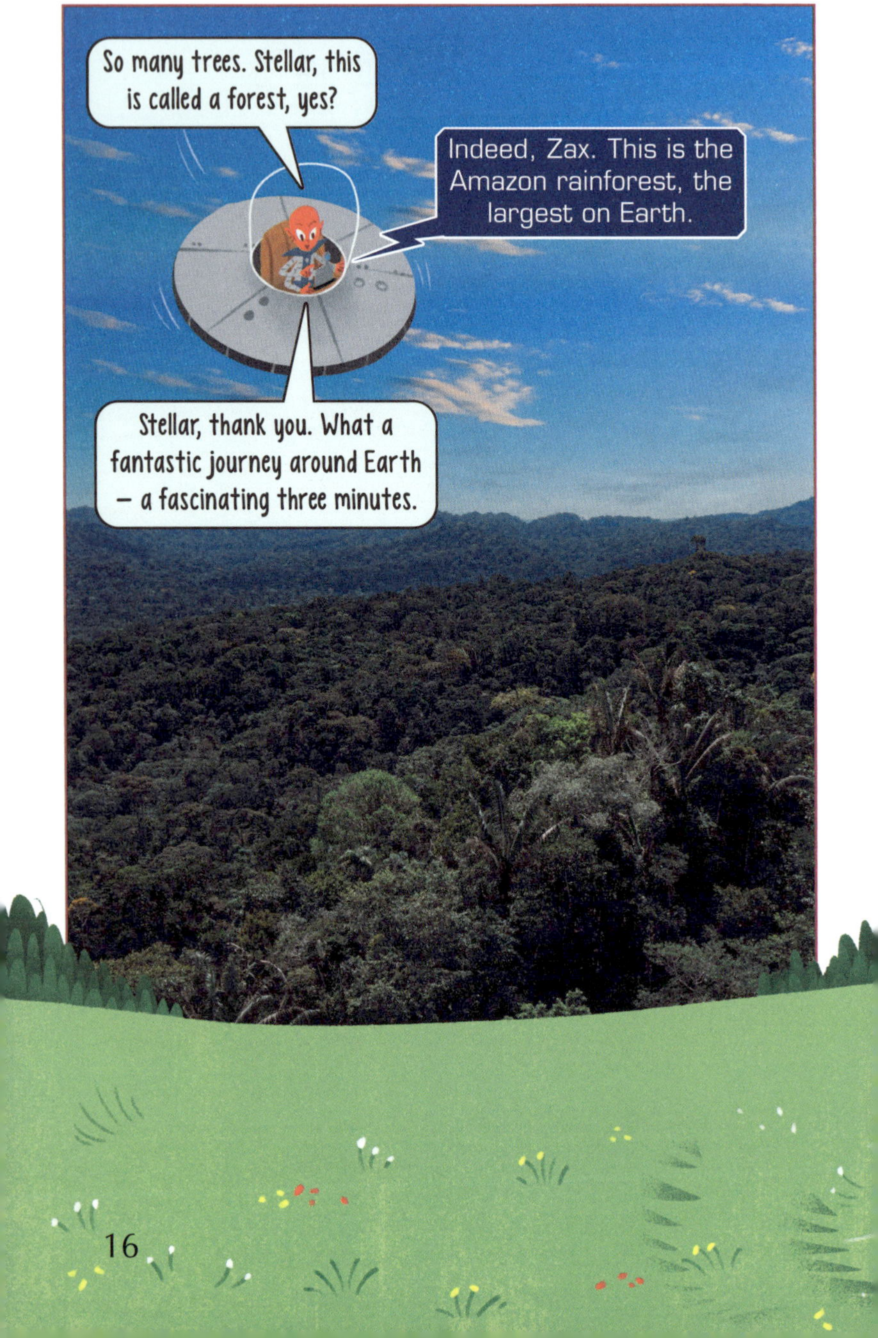
So many trees. Stellar, this is called a forest, yes?
Indeed, Zax. This is the Amazon rainforest, the largest on Earth.
Stellar, thank you. What a fantastic journey around Earth – a fascinating three minutes.

Audio Recording No. 3

Time to get on with my project.

Preparing for landing. Engage the protective bumpers.

Remember, stick to the mission. Collect a rock or two, get Grandpa's present and return to the spaceship.

I will NOT mix with Earthlings. But I WILL wear my Earthling Camouflage Suit in case I meet any.

What could possibly go wrong?

End of transmission.

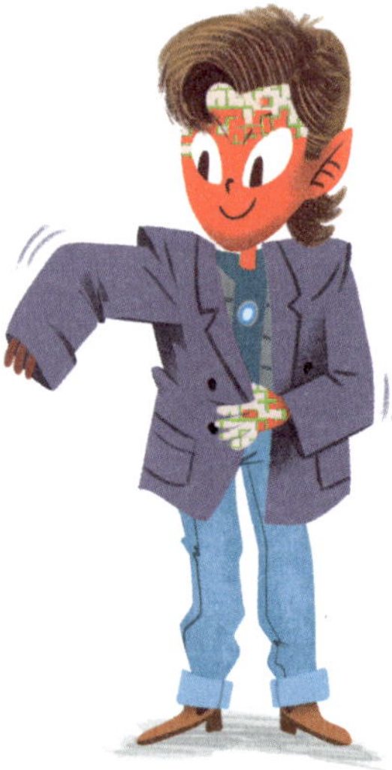

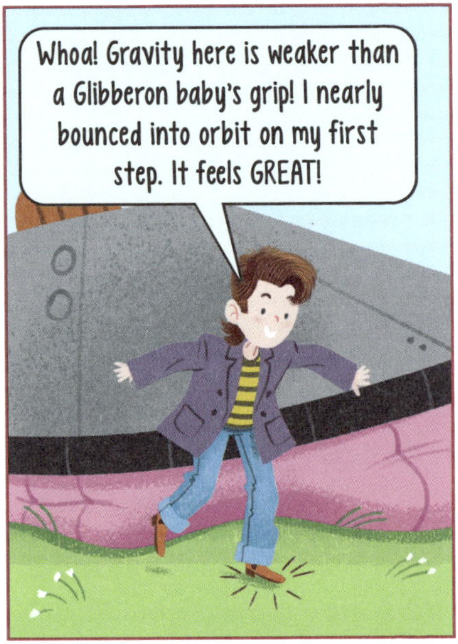
Whoa! Gravity here is weaker than a Glibberon baby's grip! I nearly bounced into orbit on my first step. It feels GREAT!

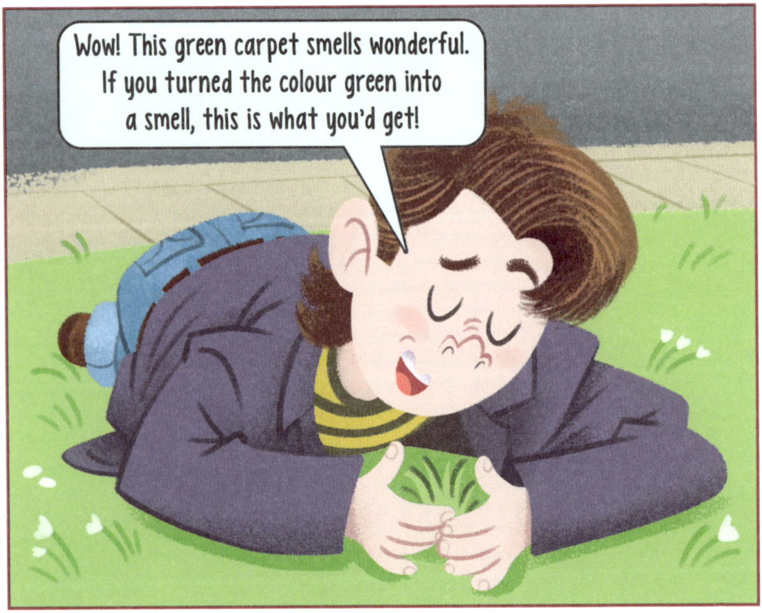
Wow! This green carpet smells wonderful. If you turned the colour green into a smell, this is what you'd get!

"And that creature smells amazing! Like Grandpa's socks and my big brother's sports bag."

"But this one is my favourite. The Earthlings are being pulled into that building by the delicious aromas. I must resist!"

BAKERY

Audio Recording No. 4

I have found the perfect spot. And I can also make Grandpa's present.

Grandpa said his favourite thing on his visit to Earth was listening to running water. He still thinks of it when he is trying to sleep. I want to record the sound for him.

Audio, set volume to maximum. And record.

Perfect. It's a very soothing sound. Grandpa will love it!

Brilliant! I've found a lovely brown Earth rock. I just need a moon rock now – that won't take long. A successful mission. And I wasn't spotted by any Earthlings … oh!

End of transmission.

Amazing Earth

Mount Everest

Mount Everest is the tallest mountain on Earth, standing at 8,849 metres tall.

And it's growing taller! Each year, Everest grows around four millimetres, as two of Earth's plates underneath the mountain push against each other.

At its summit, there is not enough oxygen for humans to breathe normally. It's also very cold and the wind can reach more than 320 kilometres per hour!

Sahara Desert

The Sahara is Earth's largest hot desert, covering an area almost as big as the United States! During the day, temperatures can reach a sweltering 56 degrees Celsius. But at night, the temperature can drop below freezing! This is because there are almost no clouds to act like a blanket, so all the daytime heat escapes into space.

Amazon rainforest

Earth's largest rainforest, the Amazon, is so big that it covers parts of NINE different countries in South America. The UK could fit into it over 25 times!

Scientists discover new plants and animals there at a rate of two or three a week!

The Amazon rainforest produces so much oxygen that it's sometimes called the 'lungs of the planet'.

CHAPTER 2

Earthlings!

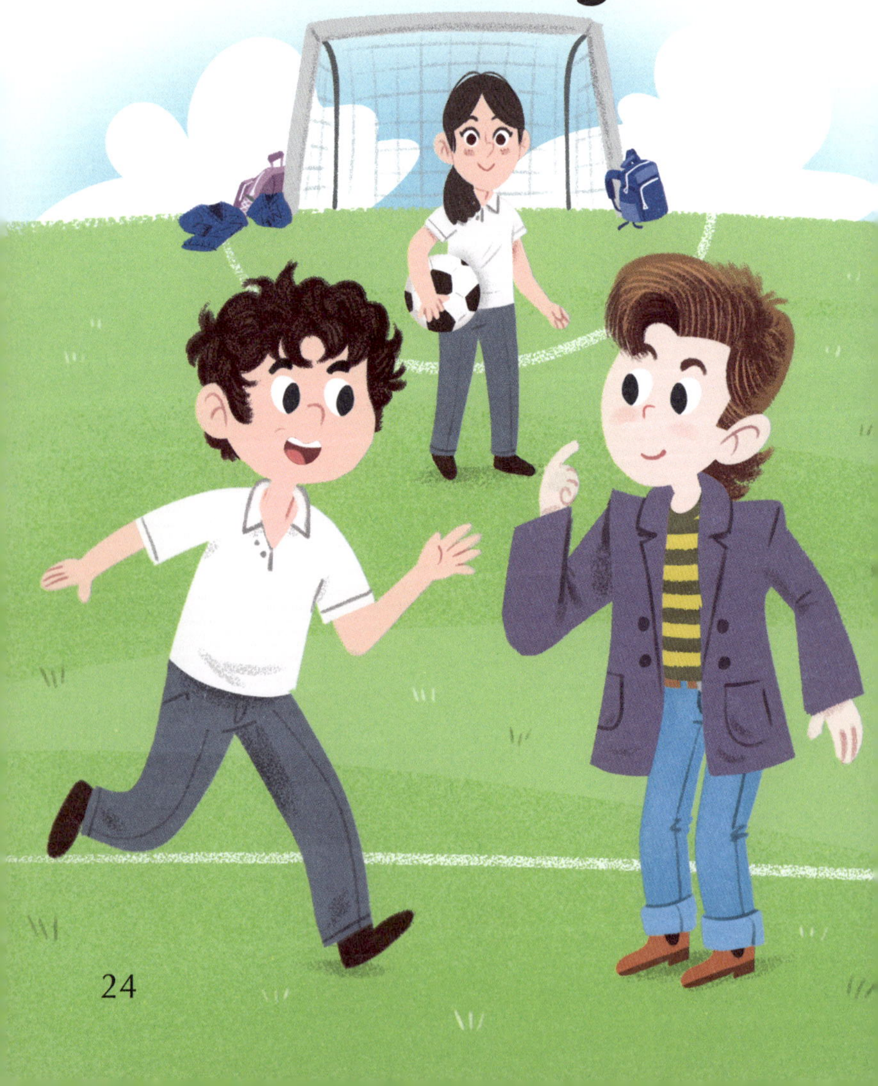

"Hey, you," says the Earthling boy. "Do you want to play?"

"Me?" I ask.

"Yes, you," says the boy. "You can go in goal."

"In goal?"

"Do you repeat everything?" asks the boy.

"Repeat everything? No."

"Good. Now just stop the ball going in the net. Got it?"

I pause to check my 1981 Earthling Manual. "Right on, dude!"

The boy looks puzzled, but there's no time to wonder why – I have a game to win!

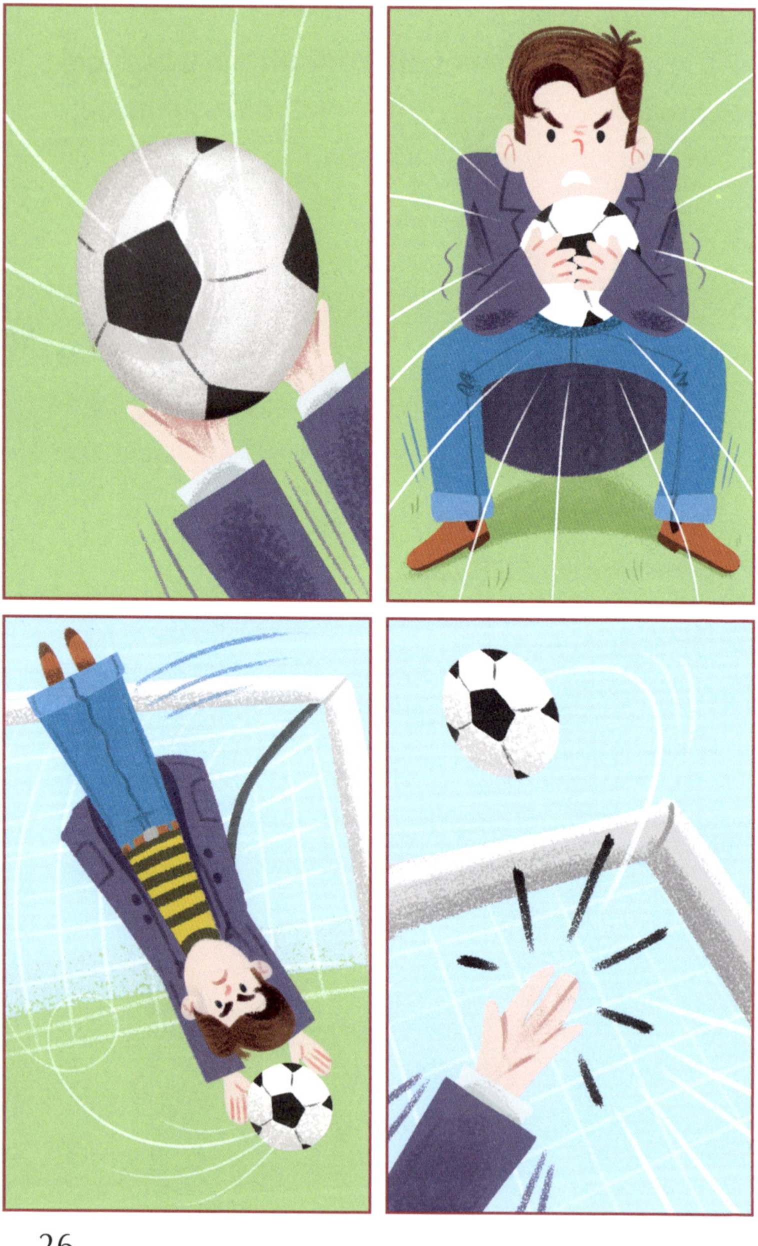

The same boy comes up to me afterwards. A girl's with him. "Wow!" says the boy. "You're amazing! What's your name? I'm Nathan."

"And I'm Aisha," says the girl.

"My name is Zax." I study the manual. "Outta sight meeting you."

Aisha looks at me curiously. "That's the first game I've played where I haven't scored," she says. "You were like a ninja."

"A ninja is good?" I ask.

"Er, yeh!" she replies.

"I found it easy," I say, surprised. "The ball didn't travel fast at all."

I look down modestly – and that's when I notice that my suit is glitching! My normal red knees are showing through!

"Hey! Are you OK?" asks Nathan. "You look kind of … sick?"

"I'm fine – " I say. "But I need to … let you into a little secret."

Aisha looks at me blankly. "What are you talking about?"

"I'm just going to say it," I blurt. "Don't scream or anything … I'm from planet Glibberon, a long way away."

"This is … AWESOME!" says Nathan. "A real-life green Alien!"

Aisha rolls her eyes. "Nathan, Zax isn't … aaa … aaa … choo!"

I can't believe what I'm seeing. "Your face just exploded and mucus the colour of my blood flew out!" I gasp. "Impressive!"

Aisha looks embarrassed. "Not impressive. Sorry. I should have put my hand over my nose and mouth to cover my sneeze."

"Sneeze?" I like this word. It's fun to say, so I say it some more. "Sneeze, sneeze, sneeze. Oh, and now your eyes are leaking. Let me check my manual."

"It's OK," says Aisha. "It's just – "

"Crying," I carry on. "You are crying because you are sad. I am sorry if I have upset you, it was not my intention … dude."

"I'm not sad," says Aisha. "I just have hay fever."

"Do you have hay fever on your planet?" asks Nathan.

"I don't think so," I say. "A fever of hay?"

"It's where you're allergic to pollen," says Aisha. "You know, the fine powder produced by plants?"

"I do not know," I say. "But there is a lot about Earth that I have yet to learn."

"Is that why you're here?" says Nathan.

"I'm here on a school project," I explain.

"A school project!" says Aisha. "We have those, too. But you could have landed anywhere on Earth and you chose HERE?"

"You have rocks and running water," I explain, pointing towards the stream.

"You came all this way to see a stream?" says Aisha.

"Yes, and I made a present for Grandpa to remind him of his Earth visit."

"Your grandpa has been to Earth?" gasps Aisha.

"Yes, but HE wasn't spotted. His suit was brand new then. I think it's showing its age. Let me try to reset it."

I press a few buttons. Amazingly, it works!

"I'd like to eat some cloud now," I say. "How do you reach them?"

For some reason, Aisha looks very surprised by my question.

"Nobody eats clouds," says Nathan. "They're just … what are they, Aisha?"

"I'm not really sure," says Aisha, "but they're definitely not for eating. Achoo! Sorry about that."

"You don't need to apologise to me," I say hastily. "I find it fascinating. Everything on Earth is. Are you OK if I do more research to add to my school project?"

"Sure," says Aisha. "We have to get our bags."

While they're gone, I take out my tablet and look up clouds. Here's what I find out!

Why can't you eat clouds?

Clouds look fluffy and yummy, but they're made of millions of tiny water droplets spread super far apart in the air. So, there's nothing solid to actually eat!

But clouds are surprisingly heavy! A cloud the size of a street on Earth can weigh as much as 500 of their cars.

How do they stay up?

Amazingly, all of that weight stays up in the sky because warm air currents keep rising from below, pushing the tiny droplets upwards faster than they can fall.

Until … sometimes the cloud gets SO big and moist that the water droplets begin sticking to each other and grow LARGER and LARGER. Then the air below can no longer hold them up and the droplets begin to fall. This is called RAIN!

Before I know it, Aisha and Nathan are back. I tell them that I'm about to go to the Moon to get some rocks.

"Seriously?" says Nathan. "The Moon?"

"Unless you have some moon rocks that you can share with me?"

"Moon rocks?" gapes Aisha. "Why would we have moon rocks?"

"Well, it's not far away. I thought maybe you got some on one of your visits. When did you go there last?"

"Huh?" says Aisha. "We've never been to the Moon!"

This puzzles me. "But when my grandpa visited, Earthlings said they would soon have flying cars, daily space rockets to the Moon and everlasting bubblegum – whatever that is. I don't see flying cars, but what about Moon visits?"

"No – only astronauts have been to the Moon," says Nathan, "in a space rocket. We don't have a rocket."

"That's a pity," I say. "I have a spaceship that I can get to the Moon in – let me check – two shakes of a lamb's tail."

"What?" giggles Aisha.

I realise my manual is way out of date, so I try again.

"I can get to the Moon in ten seconds flat."

"Really?" says Nathan. "No way! Can we come with you?"

I think about it. "I'm not sure that's allowed."

"Our bus home is in 40 minutes, Nathan," says Aisha. "We really don't have time."

I am confused. "You have plenty of time. I suppose this would make an interesting addition to my school project."

"So, Aisha, are you up for it?" asks Nathan. "Do you want to go to the Moon?"

BONUS

Earthlings: a guide for aliens

Blinks – weird rating 2/10

Earthlings' eyes open and close every few seconds. These 'blinks' keep Earthlings' eyes moist and clean. Unlike us, they don't have self-cleaning eyes.

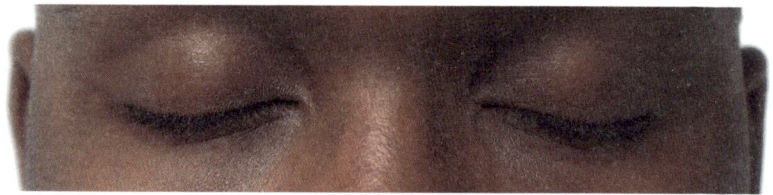

Sneezes – weird rating 5/10

Earthlings perform 'face explosions' to clear out germs from their noses; these are called sneezes. A sneeze can travel at more than 160 kilometres per hour – which is as fast as an Earthling train! It is impossible for an Earthling to keep their eyes open when they sneeze.

Yawns – weird rating 7/10

A yawn is when an Earthling suddenly opens their mouth super wide, sucks in as much air as they can and makes an 'aaaahhhh' sound. They sometimes stretch their arms. THEN … nearby Earthlings do exactly the same thing! Earthlings yawn when they are tired, or when their brains need more oxygen.

Hiccups – weird rating 10/10

These are strange and seem to serve no useful purpose. Hiccups are sudden, uncontrolled body jerks, that make Earthlings go 'HIC!'. These 'hics' happen when a muscle called the diaphragm (in their chest) gets confused and jumps around. This causes air to rush in and makes their vocal cords snap shut.

CHAPTER 3
Walking on the Moon

Audio Recording No. 5

We have landed on Earth's moon, which is called ... Moon. Very inventive.

The journey from Earth was a little bumpy for the first two seconds, then fine.

As soon as we blasted off, the Earthlings asked, "Are we nearly there yet?"

And when I said yes, the openings in their faces – let me check the name … that's it, 'mouths' – opened very wide. They both whispered, "Wow!"

The journey was so short that the Glibberon Glider never even got out of second gear.

The Earthlings are changing into the spare spacesuits. We plan on a very quick moon walk.

I will collect rocks for my school rockery. Then I'll drop the Earthlings back on their unusual planet and go straight home.

I miss you, Mum!

End of transmission.

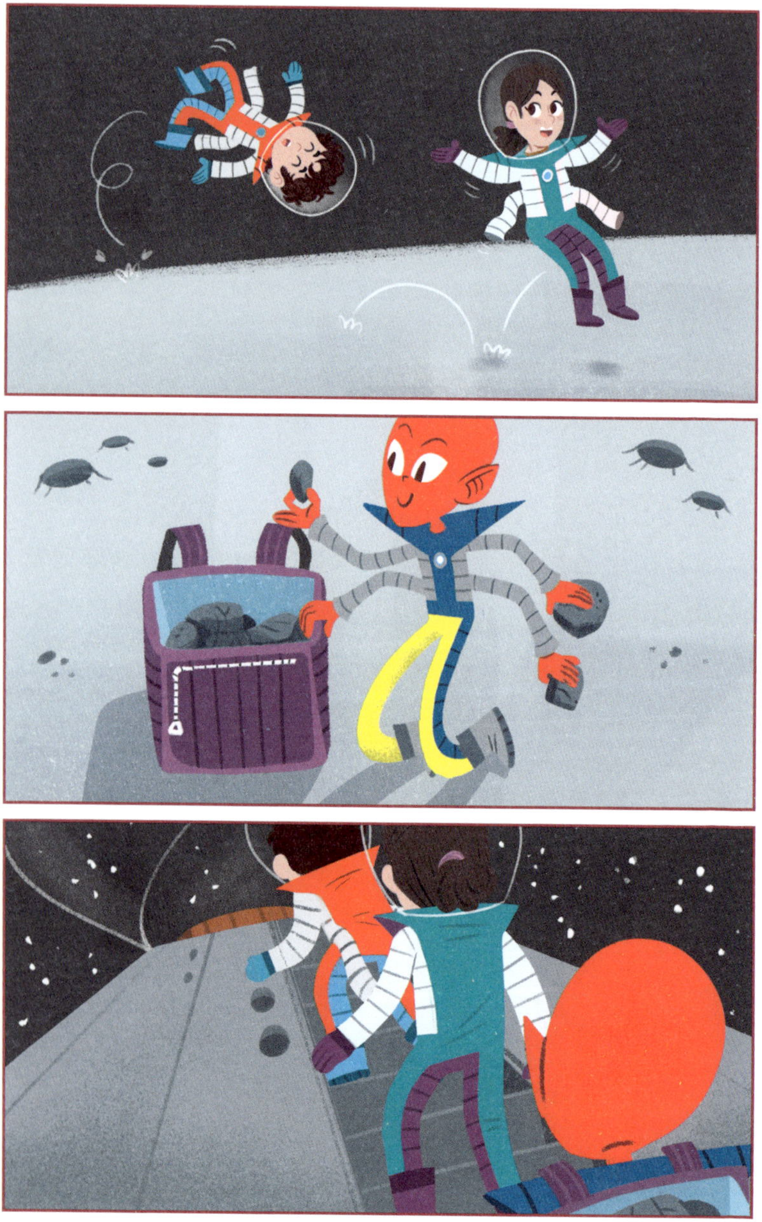

Audio Recording No. 6

Aisha and Nathan had fun bouncing on the Moon.

They were not the first Earthlings to walk on the Moon, though.

My Earthling Manual tells me the first one was an American astronaut called Neil Armstrong more than 50 Earth years ago. He called it, "One small step for a man, one giant leap for mankind." Which is smart … for an Earthling.

We found Earthling footprints on the dusty surface. They look like they were made today. That is because the Moon has no air, so there's no weather! Without wind or rain, nothing moves the dust around or causes the footprints to fade. They'll be like this for millions of years!

We also saw lots of things left behind by Earthlings: moon buggies, space boots, a shovel and even a golf ball! Nathan tells me golf is a game Earthlings play, where they try to hit a ball with a stick into a small hole in the ground ... 18 times. Apparently, this is 'fun'.

End of transmission.

Time for a bit more homework ...

Fun facts about the Moon

1 Boing-boing
The Moon's gravity is about six times weaker than Earth's. That means when humans jump on the Moon, they feel like a kangaroo … on a trampoline!

2 Hot and cold
The Moon has no air or atmosphere to block some of the Sun's rays. So, in daylight it gets up to 127 degrees Celsius – that's way hotter than the highest temperatures ever recorded on Earth (56.7 degrees Celsius). But at night, because there is no atmosphere to trap that heat, it gets colder than a snowman's toes! (minus 173 degrees Celsius)

3 Long day!

The Moon rotates REALLY slowly. It takes about 29 Earth days for one full spin. That means if you were on the Moon, daytime would last about two weeks, and night-time would also last about two weeks. Longest sleepover ever!

4 Lots of holes and one ENORMOUS crater!

The Moon has more than 300,000 craters that are wider than a kilometre – and that only includes the ones seen from Earth. The largest is the South Pole-Aitken basin which is 2,500 kilometres wide and around eight kilometres deep.

That basin is absolutely huge! If humans could drop their Eiffel Tower into it, it would be like throwing a toothpick into an empty swimming pool!

time till bus leaves

This has been a super successful mission. I have gathered some moon rocks, and the Earthlings loved being astronauts. Now it's time to take them home.

"Ready for departure back to Earth?" I say.

"Can I drive?" asks Nathan, keenly.

"I'm afraid not," I say. "You don't have enough – "

"Experience?" suggests Aisha.

"No, hands. You need two hands to steer. And two to press the controls. Total: four hands."

"WE have four hands," say Nathan and Aisha together.

I have to admit they're right. "OK," I say, "let's have a quiz. If you beat me, you can take us back to Earth."

"Game on!" says Nathan.

"Game on?" I ask.

"OK, go!" says Nathan.

I'm puzzled. "You want me to go?"

"What Nathan is trying to say," says Aisha, "is you can ask us your first question now."

"OK, Nathan," I say, "which is bigger? The Moon or Earth?"

"Easy," says Nathan. "Earth."

"Correct," I say. "How much bigger?"

"Hey, it's our turn to ask you a question," says Aisha.

"Also correct. Game on!"

Aisha doesn't waste any time. "How much bigger is Earth than the Moon?"

This is easy! "I studied this in my first year of school," I say. "Earth is 12,800 kilometres in diameter, while the Moon is 3,500 kilometres. So, Earth is roughly four times bigger than the Moon."

Aisha mutters to Nathan, but I can hear her. "We'll never beat Zax."

"Here's your question, Aisha," I say. "What is the largest area of water on your planet? I believe they are called oceans?"

Aisha seems pleased. "I know this! It's the Pacific."

"That is correct," I admit.

Aisha whispers to Nathan, "What can we ask Zax?"

"I have an idea," says Nathan. "Hey, Zax, on the Moon, what moves faster, heat or cold?"

I play for time. "Hmmm, tricky. Since there is no air and – "

"Do you give in?" says Nathan.

They've got me! I nod.

"It's heat," says Nathan. "Heat moves faster, because you can catch a cold."

"I don't understand – " I start.

"Never mind," says Nathan. "Hand us the keys!"

Audio Recording No. 7

Note to self. Never get into a quiz with Earthlings. While their 'intelligence' is limited compared to ours, they are very cunning.

Now I have to let them drive the Glibberon Glider back to Earth. But it's so easy that even young Earthlings could do it. It's not exactly rocket science, is it? What could possibly go wrong?

End of transmission.

"I can't believe I'm actually going to fly a spaceship!" says Aisha.

"Me neither," says Nathan. "I only took the stabilisers off my bike last year."

"I've switched the settings to basic," I tell them. "When I sit down, Nathan, press the big black button. Aisha, pull the steering wheel towards you."

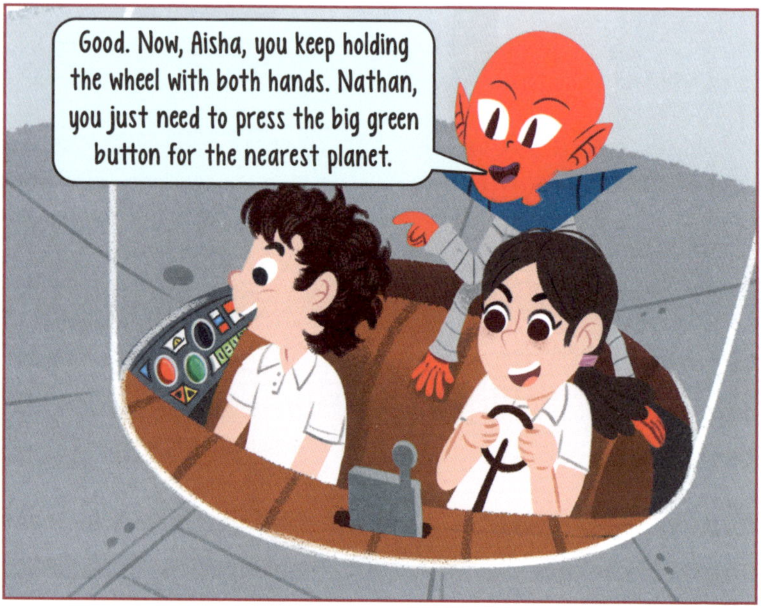
Good. Now, Aisha, you keep holding the wheel with both hands. Nathan, you just need to press the big green button for the nearest planet.

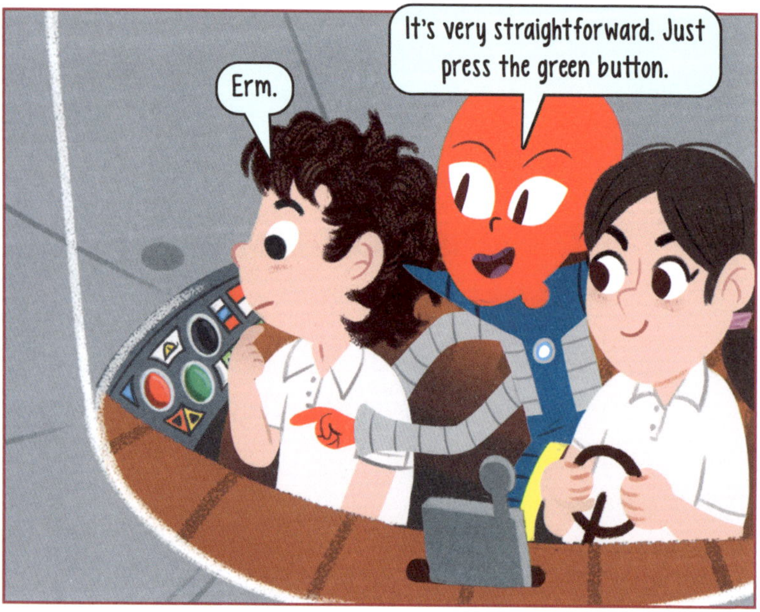
Erm.
It's very straightforward. Just press the green button.

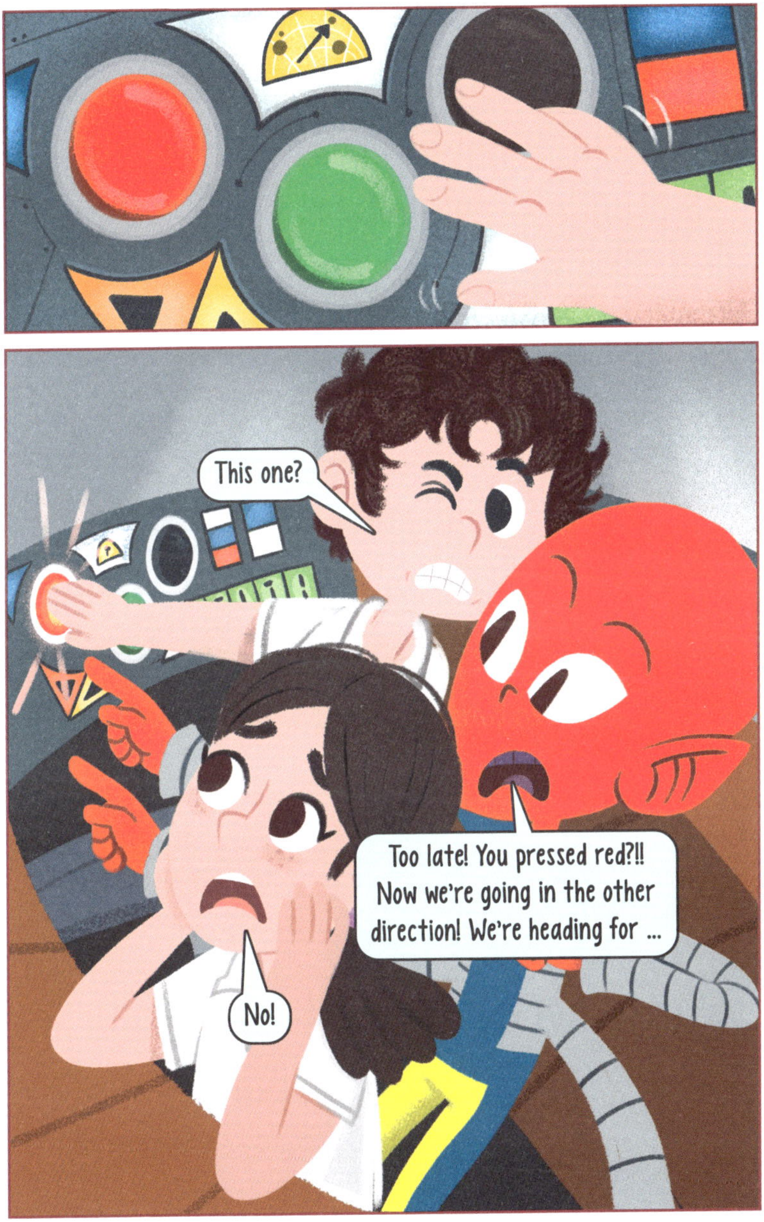
This one?
Too late! You pressed red?!! Now we're going in the other direction! We're heading for ...
No!

BONUS

Earth and the Moon

Nearly three-quarters of Earth's surface is covered in water – which is why it looks so blue from space.

There really is a dark (or far) side of the Moon for Earthlings. The Moon always faces the same way. This means that 41% (or nearly half) of the surface of the Moon can never be seen from Earth.

The Sun and the Moon are not the same size. They might look the same size from Earth, but the Moon is actually 400 times smaller than the Sun, but also 400 times closer to Earth.

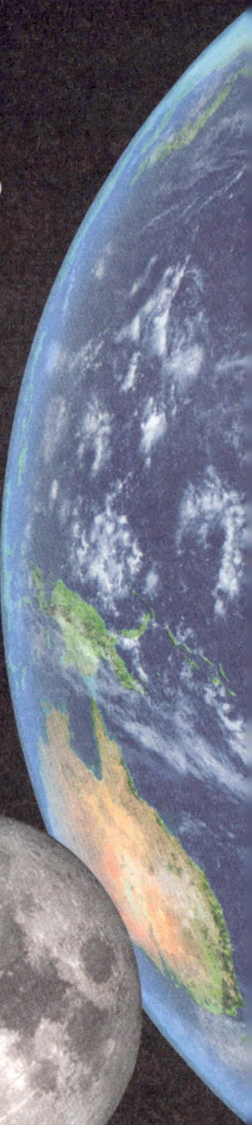

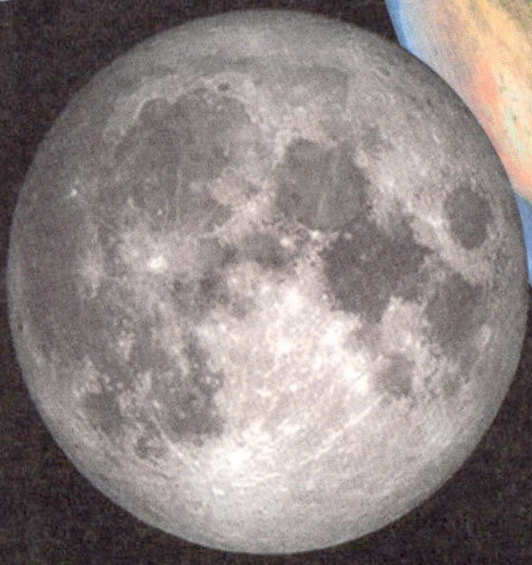

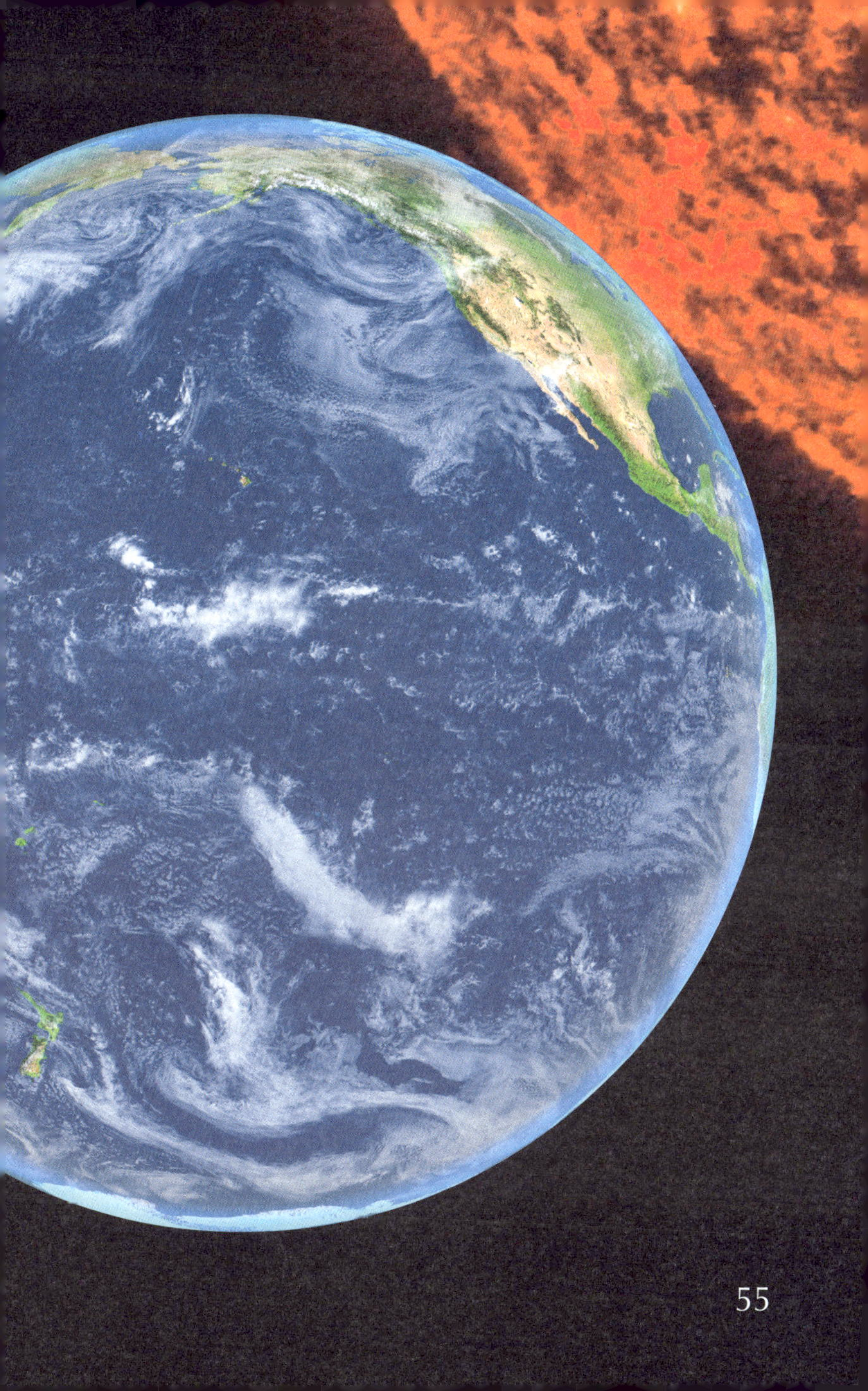

CHAPTER 4

Life on Mars

"Mars!" I yelp. "We are now heading to Mars!"

"Can't we just turn around?" asks Nathan.

I sigh. "That's not possible. We're locked on course. Let me check something. Stellar, how far away is Mars?"

Immediately, Stellar replies, "At take-off from the Moon, it was 63 million Earth kilometres away. Now it is … calculating – "

"That's good news," I say, relieved.

"63 MILLION?" says Aisha, incredulously. "And that's good news?"

"Yes. My manual tells me that Mars is often more than 200 million Earth kilometres away. This will be a much shorter journey."

There's a whirring noise. Stellar is still calculating.

"How short?" asks Nathan.

"… calculation complete," says Stellar. "Mars is now one million kilometres … no, cancel that. We have arrived."

"Wow!" says Aisha. "We're here already!"

"It's the Cosmic Crystals," I say. "Fastest fuel in the universe."

"Now that we're here," says Aisha, "can we take a quick look around?"

"I believe you have time," I say. "Nathan, would you like to step on Mars?"

"Sure," says Nathan. "It looks kind of dusty."

"And the sky is orange!" says Aisha.

Mars isn't part of my school project, but I decide to do some research anyway.

Why is the sky orange on Mars?

It's all to do with iron. Mars has lots of tiny iron particles on its surface, and over billions of years this iron has rusted (just like old metal left out in the rain). Wind picks up these tiny rusty dust particles and they float in the air. When sunlight shines through this dusty air, it makes the whole sky look orange!

Audio Recording No. 8

There is no water on Mars, unlike Earth and Glibberon. No one playing football. Or any signs of life.

Fortunately, it took us only 46 Earth seconds to get here. We should head straight back to Earth. But my Earthling friends want to explore. I, too, am curious. I could, I suppose, bring back one rock sample …

But we must hurry. I need to get my Earthlings back to their planet soon. However, one of them has put on their spacesuit back to front. Again. I will go and help them.

End of transmission.

We've finally made it outside.

"It's not as bouncy as the Moon," says Aisha, "but it's still pretty bouncy."

"That's because Mars has more gravity than the Moon," I explain. "But it's still only about a third of what you have on Earth."

"Wow!" says Nathan. "That mountain is huge!"

"We studied that at school," I say. "It's a volcano called Olympus Mons, the tallest in your solar system. It's three times bigger than your largest mountain, which – "

"Hey, Zax," Nathan interrupts. "What's the smartest mountain on Earth?"

"I don't know," I reply. "What is the smartest mountain on Earth?"

"Mount Cleverest!"

"I've never heard of that mountain. Is it near Mount Everest?"

"No, it's – " says Nathan. "Never mind."

"I have a joke for you, Nathan," says Aisha. "I checked out a book on anti-gravity. I can't put it down!"

"You Earthlings are most amusing," I say. "I also like the way you have to name everything. Even the rocks on this planet have been given names." I call over to the Glider. "Stellar, can you tell us about these names?"

Stellar's voice rings out. "Of course. Earth's first robot rover – called Sojourner – landed on Mars in 1997 and sent images back to Earth.

The scientists decided to name some of the rocks that Sojourner had discovered after famous cartoon characters.

One of the most famous rocks studied by Sojourner was named after a cartoon character, called Yogi Bear, because it looked like a bear's head from certain angles.

Then there is Scooby Doo, who is a cartoon dog. This rock had a similar shape to him.

And they have Pooh Bear. This rock was discovered near Yogi, and again it reminded one of the mission team of another famous bear.

Finally, there is a rock called Casper. This was named after a friendly ghost character. It got its name because, like ghosts which are often pale, the rock is unusually light compared to the other rocks near it."

We head back inside.

"Can you see any other planets from here?" asks Nathan.

"Is that tiny blue dot Earth?" Aisha suggests.

"Yes," I say. "And we need to head straight back there soon. You don't want to miss your bus."

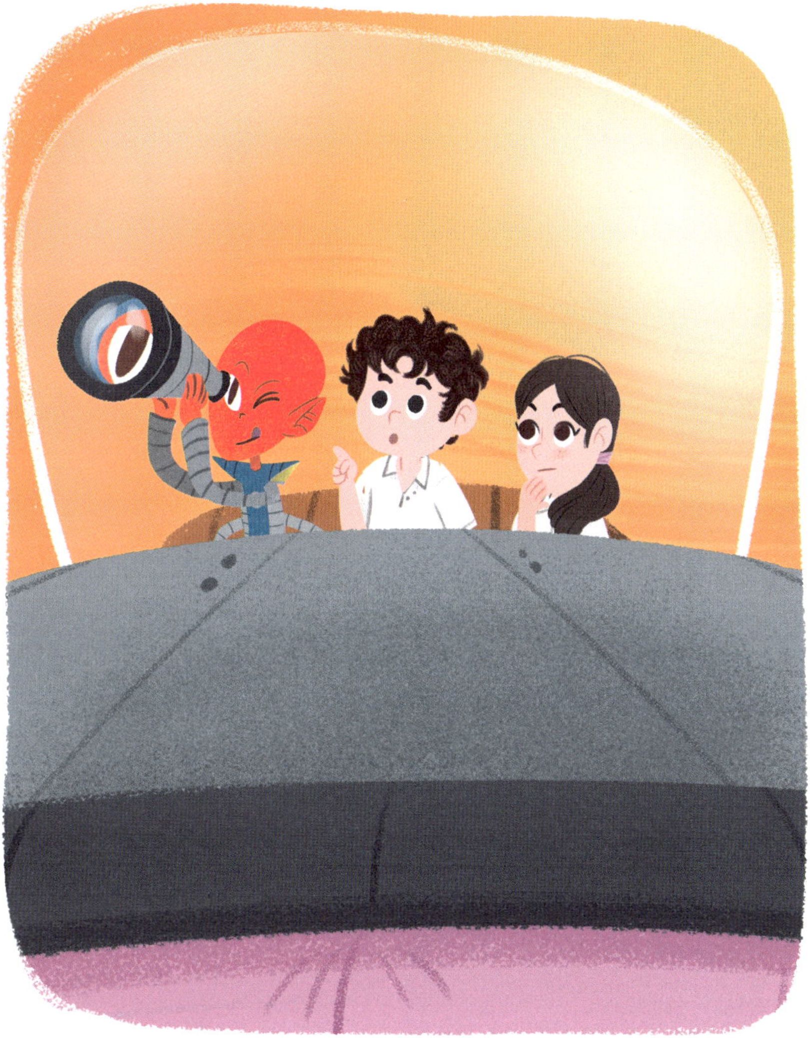

"What's that planet there?" asks Nathan, pointing.

I check it out with the telescope.

"Hmm … It's very close to the planet called Jupiter, but – "

"But?" says Aisha.

"It shouldn't be there. It's an asteroid. A big one."

"Is that like a comet?" asks Aisha.

"Yes," I reply. "It's a rocky object that orbits your Sun."

"So where's it heading for?" asks Aisha.

"Stellar," I say, "we have located an asteroid near Jupiter. We need you to tell us where it's headed."

Stellar scans space. "The asteroid is definitely going to miss Jupiter," she says. "And it's not going to collide with Mars … or the Moon … oh."

"Oh? Stellar, what does 'oh' mean?" asks Nathan.

"You are Earthlings, correct?" says Stellar.

Nathan and Aisha both answer together: "Yes."

"Then I regret to inform you," says Stellar, "the asteroid is heading straight for Earth!"

"When will it get there?" asks Aisha.

"At the speed it is travelling, assuming a constant rate – "

"WHEN!" chorus Aisha and Nathan.

"28 Earth years, five months, four days, six minutes and 19 seconds," replies Stellar.

"Phew!" says Nathan. "That's a long time."

"In Earth years, yes," I say. "But the closer the asteroid gets to Earth, the harder it will be to stop it."

"Well, how big is it?" asks Nathan. "Is it the size of a football stadium?"

"Bigger," I say.

"How big?" asks Nathan.

"It is the size of your Earth city, London."

"Wow!" says Nathan.

"But as we saw from the Moon," says Aisha, "most of Earth's surface is water. It'll probably land in the ocean."

"With a big splash!" adds Nathan.

"That is a possibility. But that would cause the biggest tsunami or wave ever seen on your planet. It would wash away most of the land on Earth."

"Oh," says Nathan.

"So," says Aisha, "what do we do?"

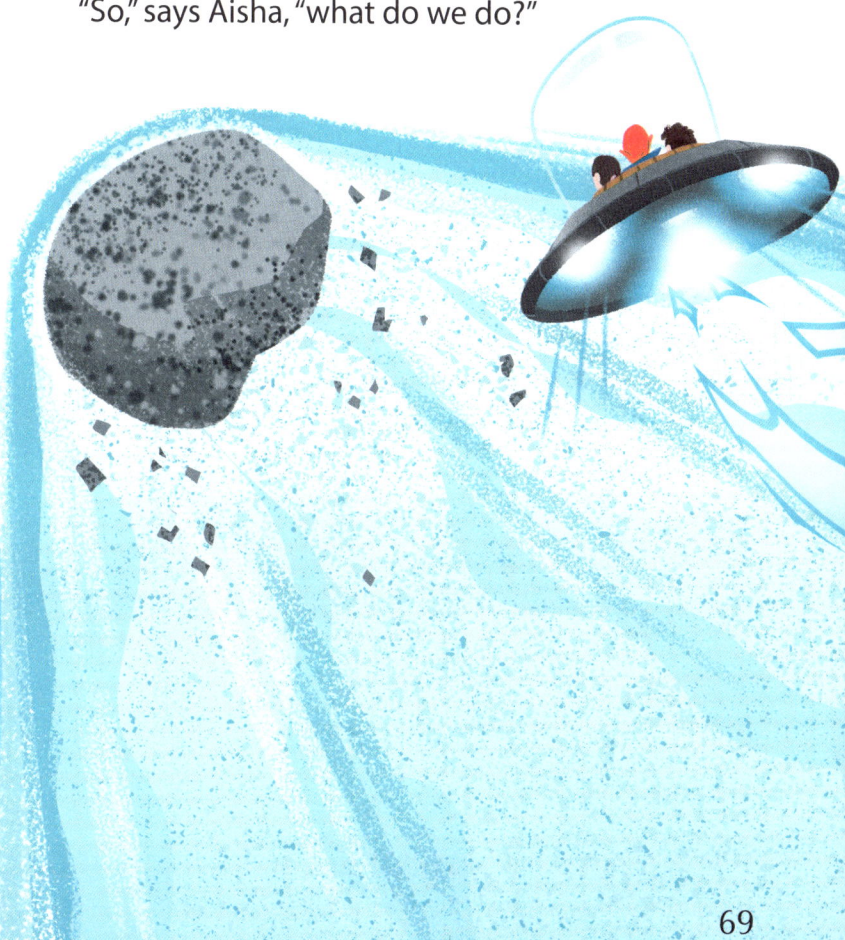

How far away is the Moon?

BONUS

The Moon is 385,000 kilometres from Earth.

If you could walk there, and you walked for ten hours every day, it would take you more than 22 YEARS to reach the Moon.

You would definitely have outgrown your shoes by then! Ouch!

If you could drive there non-stop at 80 kilometres per hour, it would take more than six MONTHS.

Don't forget snacks!

If you could fly an aeroplane there at 965 kilometres per hour, you would touch down on the Moon in about 16 days.

A space rocket will get you to the Moon in three days!

Rockets can travel at up to 40,000 kilometres per hour.

CHAPTER 5

Danger!

"I'm sure the scientists on Earth will be aware of this asteroid and have a plan," says Aisha, quietly.

"That's possible," I say. "But they may not have spotted it yet. And when they do, it might be too late."

"Can you stop the asteroid, Zax?" asks Aisha.

"Stop it? No. It's moving too quickly and it's too big. But we may be able to deflect it. Just a tiny amount. And that could be enough."

"And to do that, we need to get close to the asteroid?" asks Aisha.

"Correct."

"And how far away is it?"

"It's next to Jupiter, so 500 million Earth kilometres away. Give or take."

"This spaceship is really fast," says Nathan. "So, how long will it take?"

"At maximum speed, I estimate 400 Earth seconds," I say. "Give or take."

"That sounds a lot," says Nathan, gloomily.

"It's six minutes and 40 seconds," says Aisha. "We have to try."

time till bus leaves

Audio Recording No. 9

We have decided we must save Earth! To do that we need to deflect the asteroid off its current course.

Or, as Nathan said, "We have to knock that big rock out of the way!"

We are about to blast off. I will think of a plan on the way.

I didn't tell the Earthlings we have to cross the asteroid belt to get there. I didn't wish to alarm them. And the Glibberon Glider is excellent at dodging space rocks. Mostly.

End of transmission.

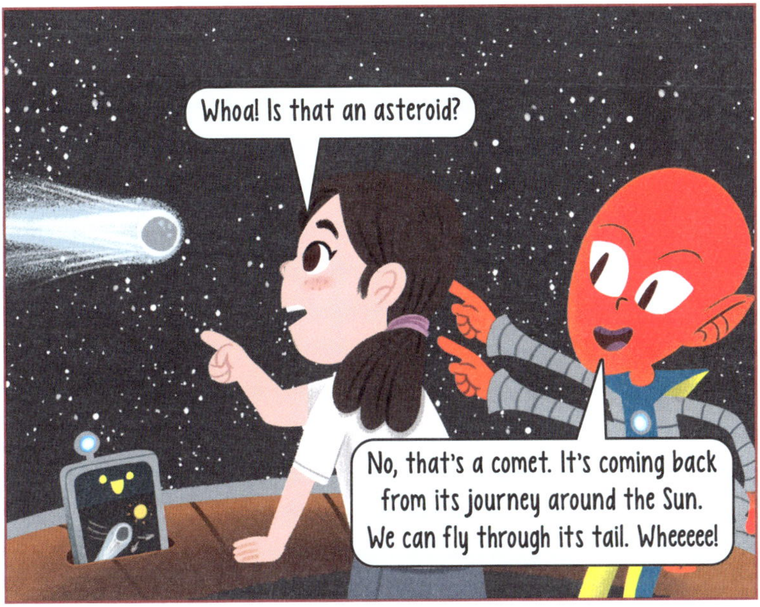
Whoa! Is that an asteroid?
No, that's a comet. It's coming back from its journey around the Sun. We can fly through its tail. Wheeeee!

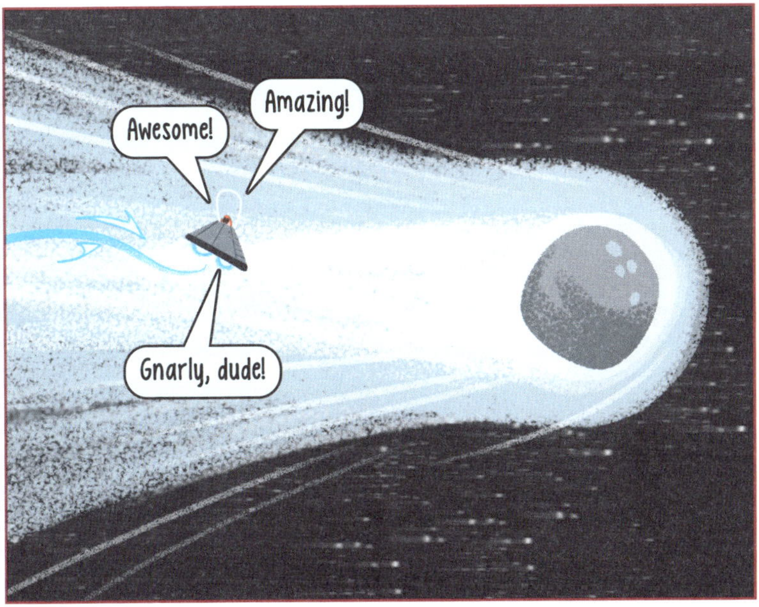
Awesome!
Amazing!
Gnarly, dude!

"Stellar," I say, "can you tell us some fun facts about comets to pass the time on this journey?"

"I can," says Stellar. "A comet is like a giant dirty snowball flying in space. They are made of ice, rocks and dust.

Some comets are as big as a small Earth city. Others are only 100–200 metres wide.

When comets get close to the Sun, their ice turns into gas, creating a glowing tail that can stretch longer than 160 million kilometres – that's longer than the distance between Earth and the Sun!

Comets have two tails – one made of glowing gas that looks blue and is straight, and another curved tail made of dusty sparkles.

A comet's head (called a coma) gets bigger as it approaches the Sun. The coma is like a glowing cloud and can become ENORMOUS – sometimes larger than most planets!

Scientists believe that comets may have brought some of Earth's water when they crashed into the planet billions of years ago. That means some of the water you drink at home, Aisha and Nathan, might once have been part of a comet!

Most comets do not get too close to the Sun. But some comets, called 'sun-grazers', crash right into the Sun and are destroyed, or get so close that they break apart from the heat."

Audio Recording No. 10

I've been thinking hard about a plan to divert the asteroid. If I remember my nursery school Astrophysics class correctly, I believe I can use reflective paint on the asteroid. This will reflect the Sun's light, altering the asteroid's path.

Here's hoping Plan A works. I have no Plan B.

I'll tell Aisha and Nathan the plan. They'll love it.

End of transmission.

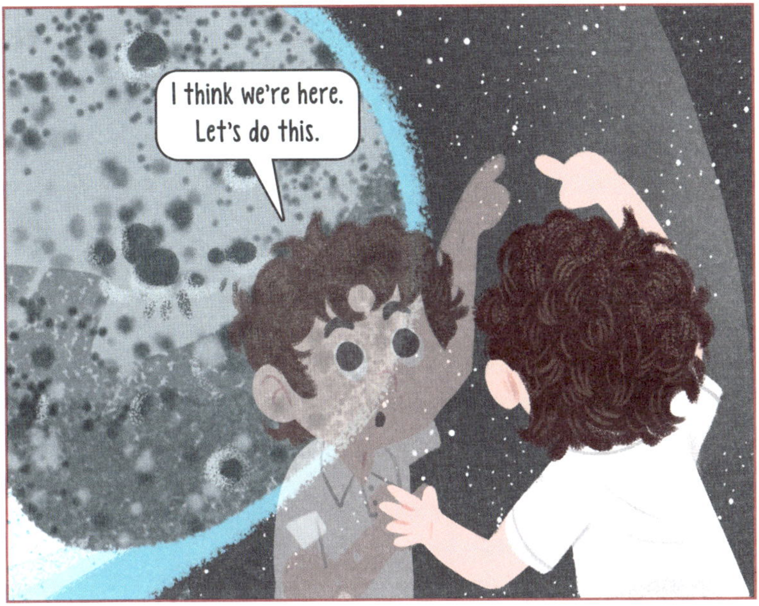
I think we're here.
Let's do this.

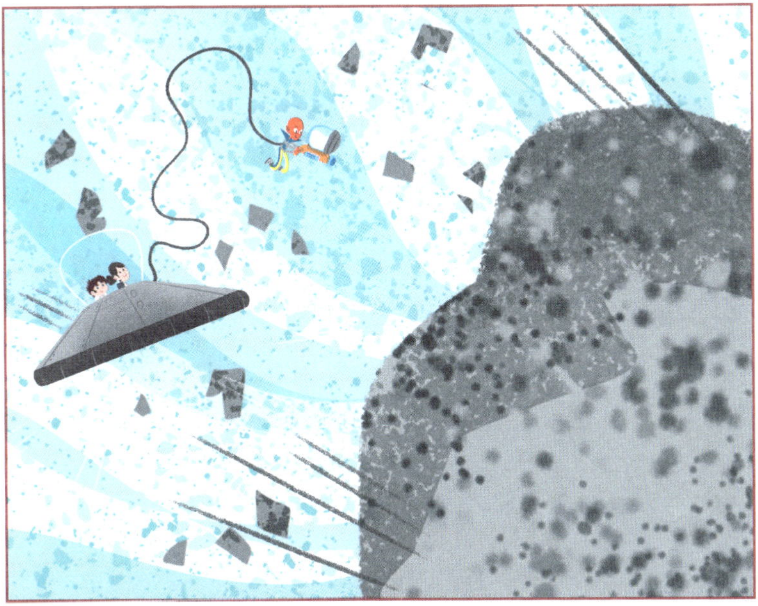

Audio Recording No. 11

We will need a Plan B, after all.

Plan A did not go well.

I fired the paint. It floated away in zero gravity. I KNEW there was something I'd forgotten from my Astrophysics class.

Whatever we decide, we need to hurry, or they will definitely miss their bus! And Earth might be destroyed. No pressure!

End of transmission.

time till bus leaves

Nathan has an idea. "Can't you just blast the asteroid? You know, with a missile?"

"We are a peaceful species," I explain. "We don't use missiles, or anything like that."

Then Aisha has a brainwave. "Nathan, you know you said the bumpers on this spaceship look just like a dodgem car?"

Nathan nods.

"Well, do you think we could bump into the asteroid and knock it off course?"

"It's a bit … erm … big!" says Nathan. "WAY bigger than this spaceship."

"What do you think, Zax?" Aisha persists. "I'm sure I read something about a small object being able to move a larger one if it hits it hard enough."

I ponder this. "If we just touched the asteroid with the front bumper of the spaceship and then switched to maximum power, it should generate a lot of force. It might work."

"We wouldn't have to nudge it far," says Aisha. "Just a little."

"Correct," I say. "Stellar, can you calculate how far we would have to push the asteroid to make sure it misses Earth?"

"Yes, I can," says Stellar.

"Hello? Stellar?" I say.

"You asked if I can calculate how far you would have to push the asteroid," says Stellar. "I can. You need to be specific."

"Stellar, how far would we have to push the asteroid to make it miss Earth?"

"It would need only a slight deviation at this distance to send the asteroid off its current course," says Stellar. "A one-degree shift would be sufficient."

"And, Stellar, can we generate that force?"

Stellar thinks about it. "I would need to know the exact density of the asteroid," she says. "But if you found its weakest point, the force from the Glibberon Glider might be enough."

"Might?" says Aisha.

"Might is better than 'not a chance,'" says Nathan. "I say we go for it."

"Me too," says Aisha. "Zax? We all need to agree."

"I admire your Earthling optimism," I say. "Let's do it."

"Let's go find your weak spot, asteroid," says Aisha.

We approach the asteroid.

"Here!" says Aisha. "There's a crack wider than a motorway."

"Perfect!" I say. "Great work, Aisha. When we touch the asteroid on the edge of that crack, Nathan, you need to press the red button. Ready?"

"There's something I have to tell you," says Nathan.

"Can it wait?" I say impatiently.

"No," says Nathan. "It can't."

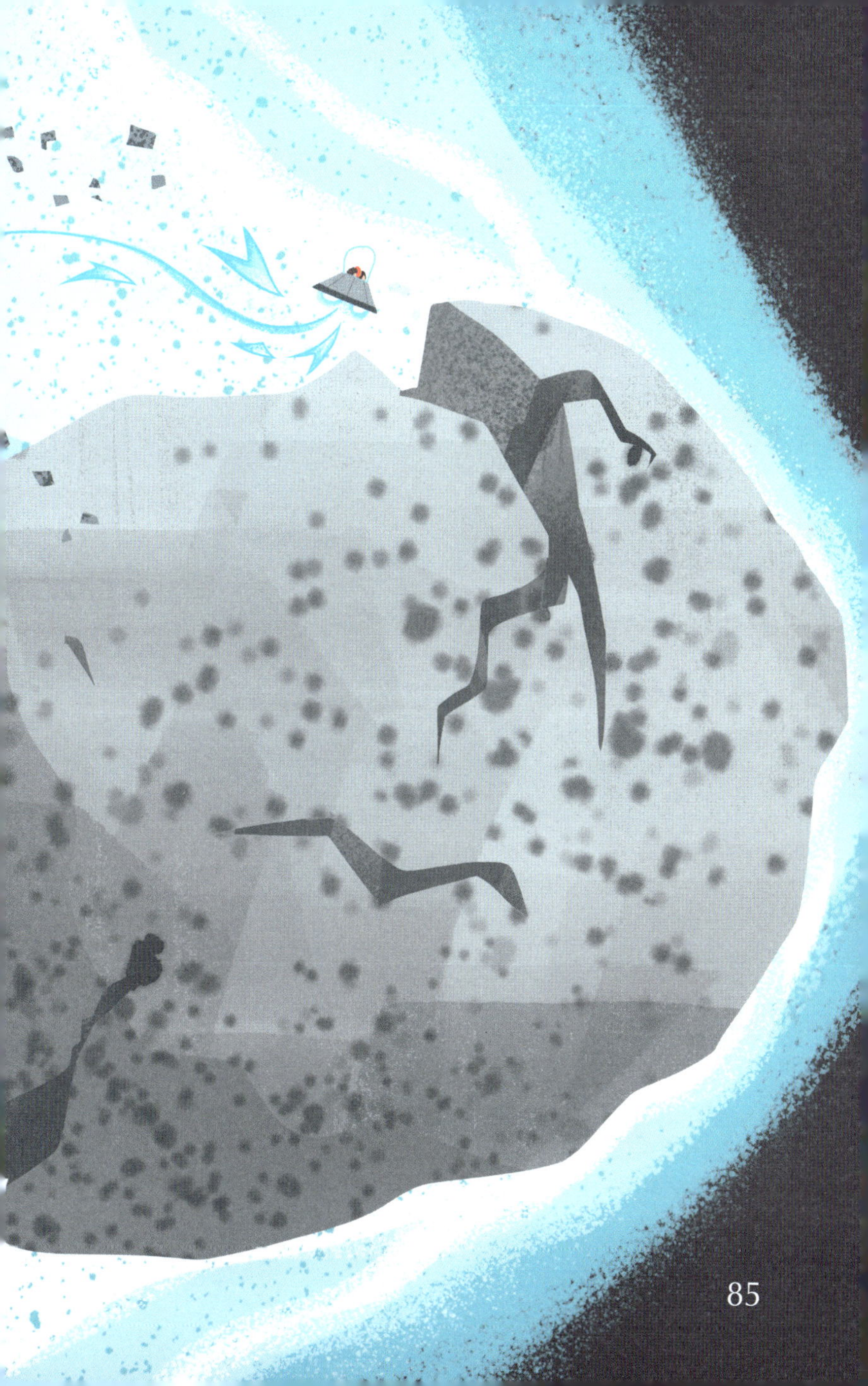

BONUS

The asteroid belt

Asteroids are rocky objects that orbit the Sun. While they can be found throughout the solar system, most are concentrated in the asteroid belt between Mars and Jupiter.

More than 600,000 asteroids in the belt have been spotted and named by Earthlings.

Most of the asteroids in the belt are no bigger than a pebble!

The largest asteroid ever spotted is Ceres and it's nearly one THOUSAND kilometres wide! That is almost as long as the whole of the UK.

Ceres

Fortunately for Earthlings, space agencies keep track of asteroids that come close to Earth.

In September 2022, NASA deliberately crashed a spacecraft into an asteroid! The plan wasn't to destroy the asteroid, but to slightly change its path – like playing cosmic bumper cars! It worked, proving that Earthlings could potentially deflect an asteroid if they needed to in the future.

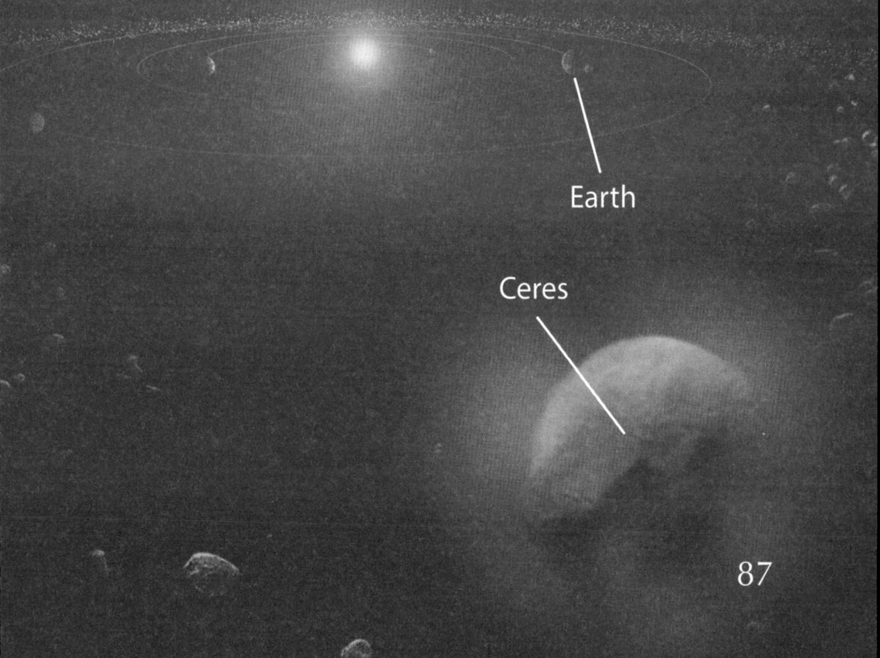
Earth
Ceres

CHAPTER 6

A race against time

Nathan has something important he needs to say.

"So, what is it, Nathan?" I ask.

"I can't tell the difference between green and red," says Nathan.

"Earthlings' eyes are not all the same?" I say, surprised.

"No," says Nathan. "I was born with colour vision deficiency."

"I never knew," says Aisha. "But I did wonder when you said Zax was green."

"It's not something you shout about," says Nathan. "The teachers know, but not many other people."

"OK," says Aisha. "We need to get this absolutely right, so this might help."

"Yes, that's helpful," says Nathan.

"If the sticker falls off," says Aisha, "remember, the red button is on the left."

"Which one is left?" says Nathan.

"Seriously?" says Aisha.

"No. Just messing with you!"

"Are you ready now, Nathan?" I ask.

"Ready," says Nathan.

"I'm so nervous, I'm sweating," says Aisha. She mops her brow with a hankie.

"Steady now," I say. "Ready to engage asteroid."

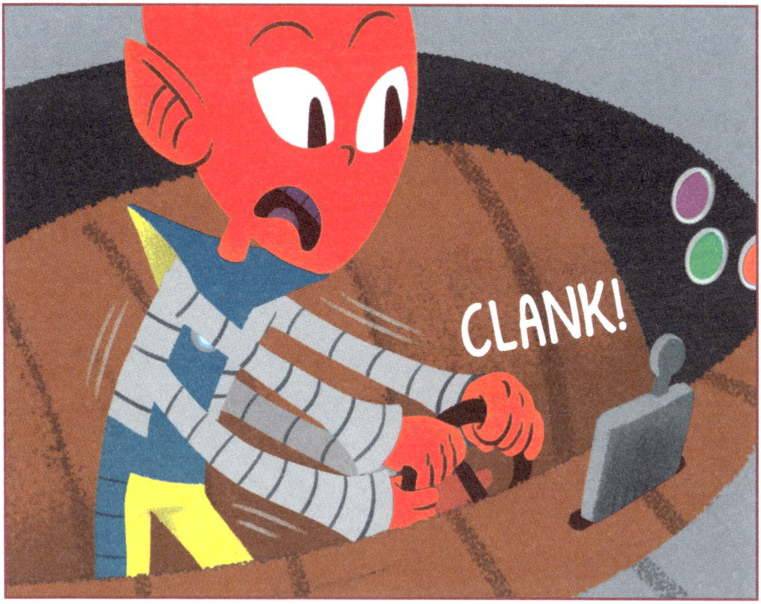
CLANK!

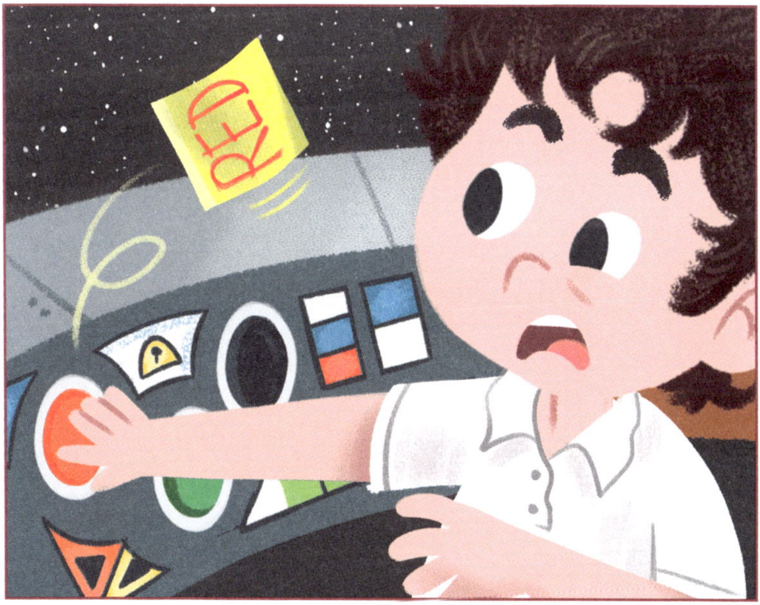
RED

"Sorry!" says Aisha. "There must have been pollen on my hankie."

"We can't stop now!" I say. "Hold tight, everyone!"

SCREEEK!

"BULLSEYE!" says Stellar. "You found the weak spot. Asteroid deflected from its path to Earth."

"Get in!" cheers Nathan.

"We did it!" yells Aisha.

"Congratulations, my super Earthling friends," I say. "You have saved your planet. Now let's get you home in time for your bus."

Audio Recording No. 12

I will take Aisha and Nathan home. I have to.

But I have a big problem. I don't even want to think about it.

I must distract myself.

End of transmission.

"I love the view of Earth from space," I say.

"It's awesome," agrees Aisha. "All that blue."

"Yes," says Nathan. "And all the red as well."

"Erm … Nathan," says Aisha.

"It's not red, is it?" says Nathan.

"Nathan, it's whatever colour you want it to be," says Aisha.

Nathan makes a funny sound, and he's smiling.

"What's that noise?" I ask. "It's very pleasant."

"It's called a laugh," says Aisha, surprised. "Have you not heard it before?"

"I heard you both performing a laugh on the Moon when you were bouncing," I say. "But the sound was muffled by your helmets."

Now Aisha is doing a laugh even more.

"I like your phrase, 'performing a laugh,'" says Aisha. "It made me … laugh!"

Earthlings really are strange.

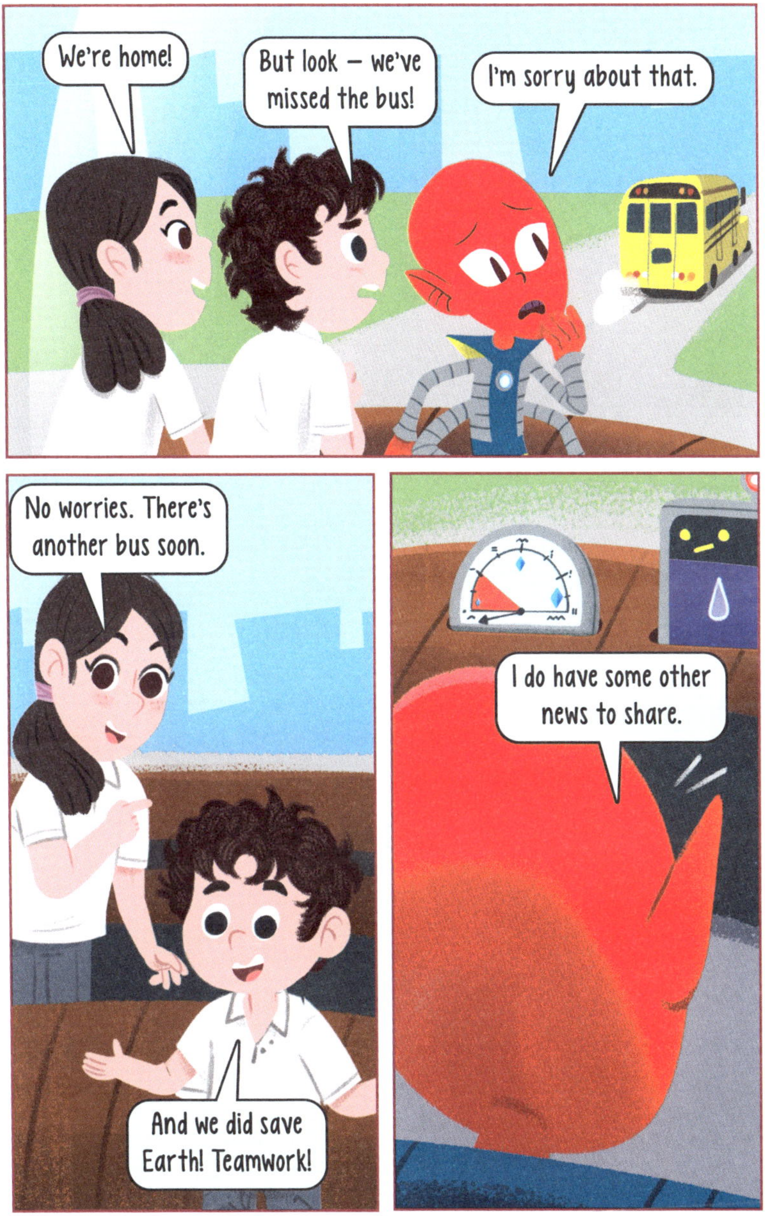

We're home!
But look – we've missed the bus!
I'm sorry about that.
No worries. There's another bus soon.
And we did save Earth! Teamwork!
I do have some other news to share.

Audio Recording No. 13

I told Aisha and Nathan that the Cosmic Crystals had run out. Which means … I can't return home. They asked if I could call my mum to come and pick me up. When I told them it wasn't possible, they both went quiet.

But I am from Glibberon. I will come up with a plan to get home. This looks like a large problem. So, I'll break it down into small pieces. Exactly two pieces. I need to find two Cosmic Crystals to fuel my spaceship and take me home.

End of transmission.

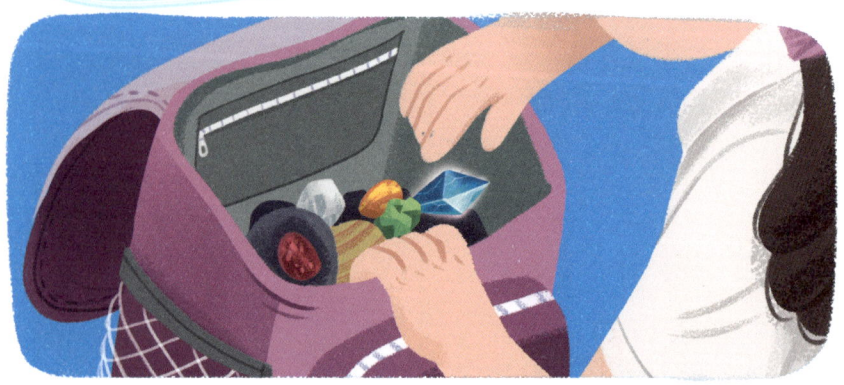

Aisha tries to take my mind off the problem. "Do you want to see my gem collection that I took into school today for show and tell?" she asks.

"Of course," I say. "Aah, these colours remind me of home."

"This is my favourite crystal," says Aisha. "It belonged to my dad. He gave it to me on my ninth birthday, because he said he found it on his ninth birthday in 1981. Apparently, he saw a UFO take off from the forest. So, he went to investigate, and he found this."

"Aisha," I say, "that's AMAZING!"

"I know!" says Aisha. "My dad and his stories!"

"No, THIS is really amazing!" I say. "Do you know what this is?"

"A gemstone," says Aisha.

"No, it's a COSMIC CRYSTAL!" I say. "Rocket fuel!"

Aisha shakes her head disbelievingly. "No way!"

"Yes," I say, "and if there's one, there may be others. I only need one more."

"Wow!" says Nathan. "I wish I had one to give you. The best I can offer you is some chewing gum. We don't have everlasting bubblegum, Zax, but this flavour is pretty neat." He hands me a thin rectangular thing.

"You are kind, Nathan," I say. "Do I ingest this?"

"No, don't swallow it. You chew it."

"Thank you," I say. "It's certainly very tasty."

"It even whitens your teeth," says Nathan.

"What?" I rush to the mirror. "Argh! My teeth are meant to be purple!"

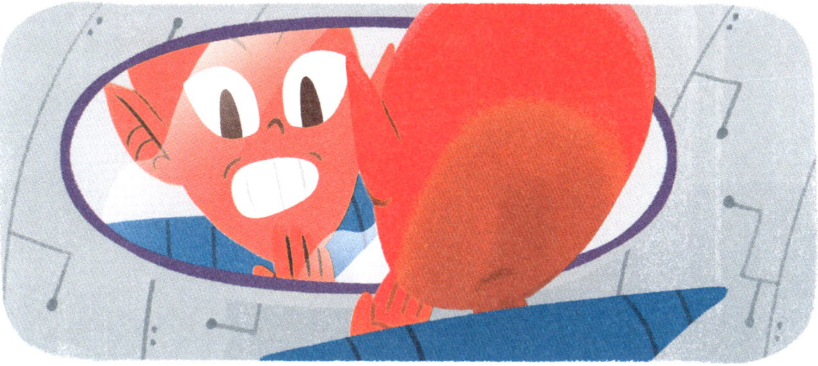

"Oops," says Nathan. "I'm sure it'll just brush off."

"Probably," I say. "I'll brush my teeth. Mum will be pleased, anyway."

While I'm brushing my teeth, I do some quick research on Earthling teeth.

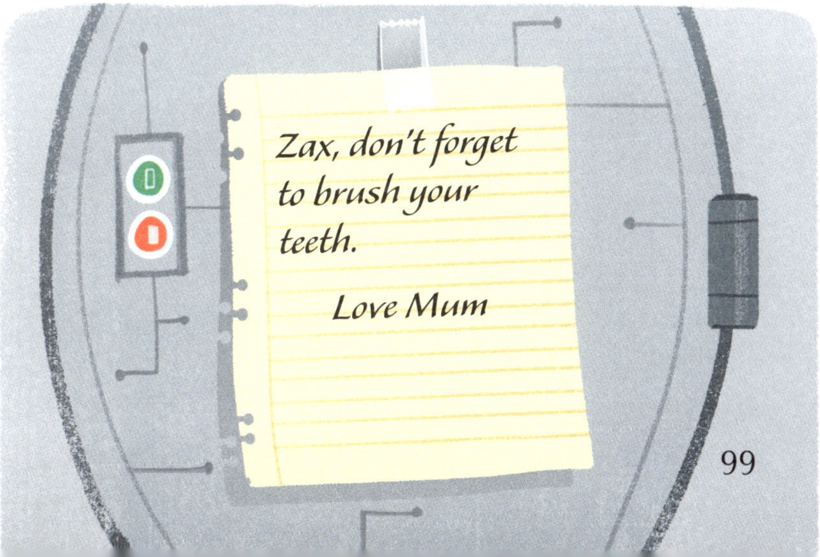
Zax, don't forget to brush your teeth.
Love Mum

Earthling teeth are coated in enamel. This is the hardest substance in the Earthling's body.

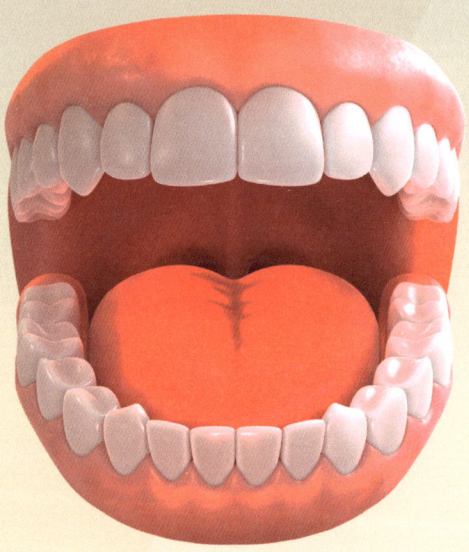

Their teeth are as unique as their fingerprints. No two Earthlings have the same teeth – not even twins.

Earthling teeth are alive! Inside each tooth is a nerve and blood vessels.

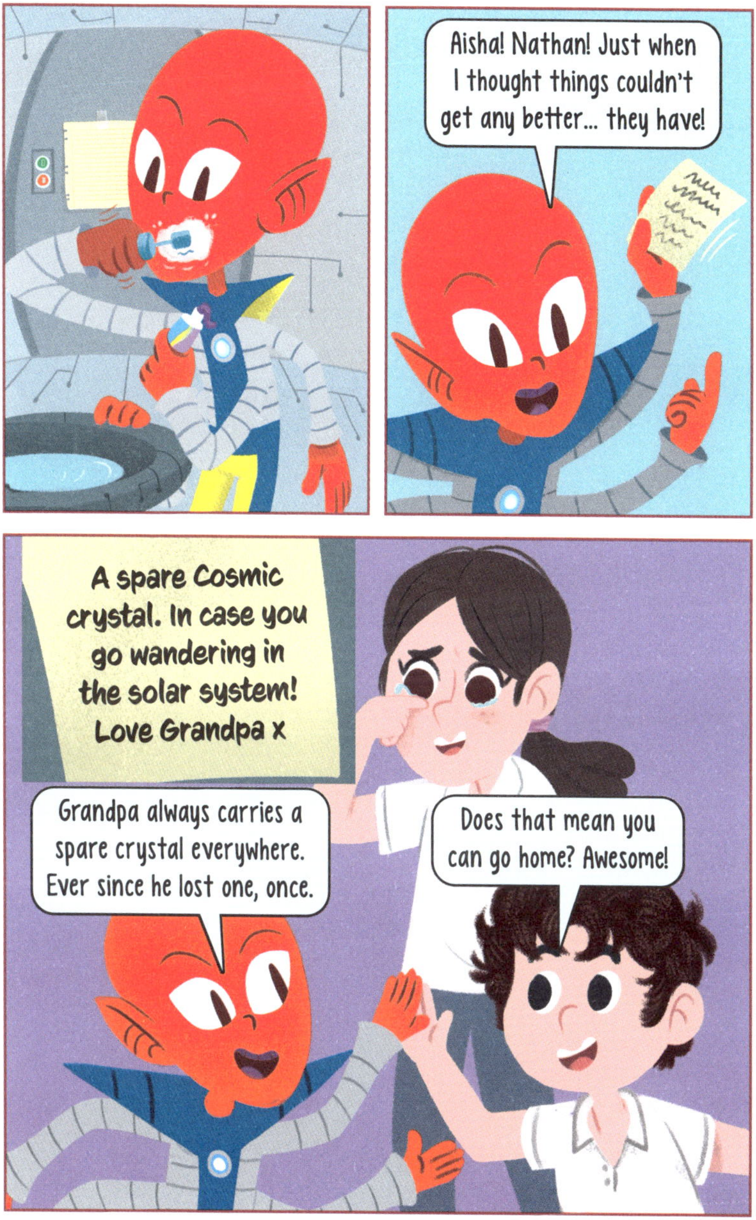
Aisha! Nathan! Just when I thought things couldn't get any better... they have!
A spare Cosmic crystal. In case you go wandering in the solar system! Love Grandpa x
Grandpa always carries a spare crystal everywhere. Ever since he lost one, once.
Does that mean you can go home? Awesome!

"Aisha," I say, "your hay fever is making your eyes water."

"It's not hay fever," says Aisha.

"Oh, then you must be sad."

"I'm sad that you're leaving," says Aisha, "but also happy that you get to go home. Your mum will be missing you."

"Don't be sad. Now I know the way here, I'll come back and see you both very soon."

Audio Recording No. 14

My school project is complete. Moon rocks really are a funky grey colour. And Earthlings are fascinating. And I may even be home in time for supper. See you again, Earth.

End of transmission.

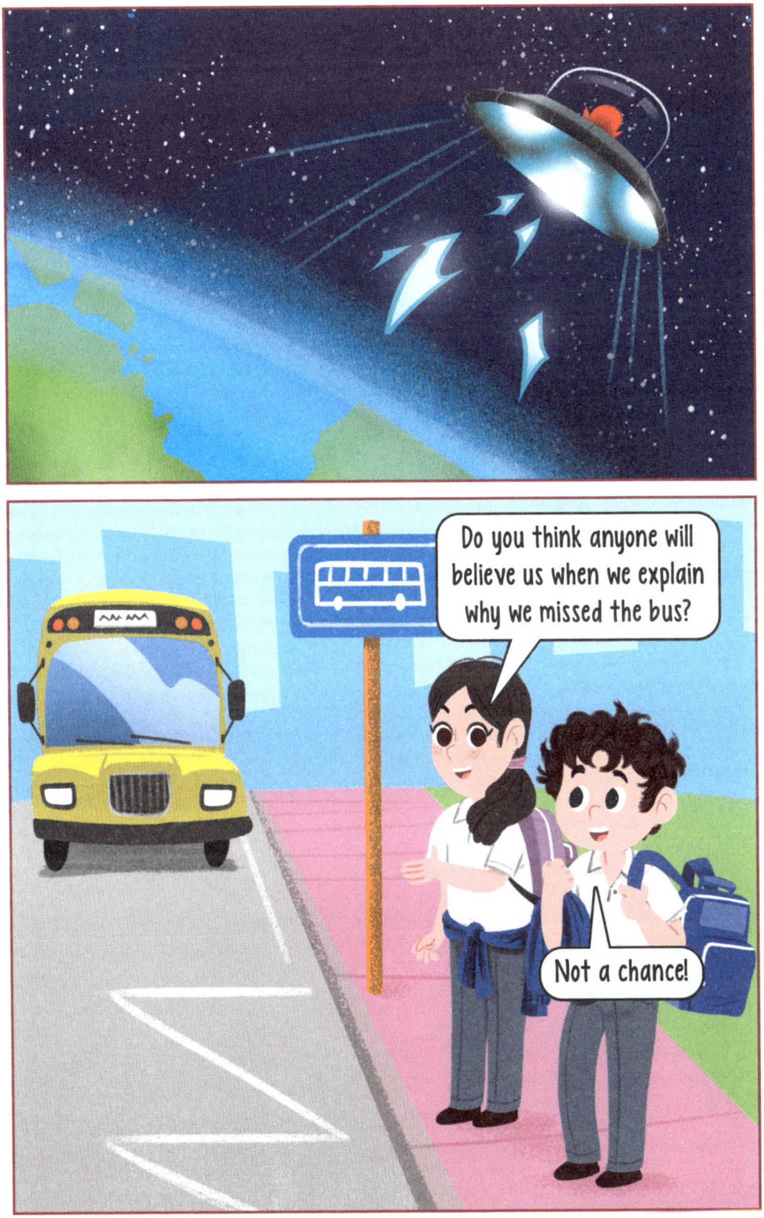
Do you think anyone will believe us when we explain why we missed the bus?
Not a chance!

Time on Earth

Why is a year 365 days?

It takes Earth just over 365 days to complete a full circle (orbit) around the Sun.

Why is there night and day on Earth?

While Earth is travelling around the Sun, it is also spinning like a top. Each spin takes 24 hours which gives Earth one day and one night.

For the side of Earth facing the Sun that's daytime, and for the side facing away, there's no light, and that's night-time.

Why is there a winter and summer?

During summer in the Northern Hemisphere, the North Pole is tilted towards the Sun. That means it gets more sunlight. In fact, in summer, the North Pole gets sunlight almost all of the time – Earthlings call this the Midnight Sun.

At the exact same time, the South Pole is tilted AWAY from the Sun. This means it's getting very little or no sunlight at all. Which makes it dark and cold in the Southern Hemisphere's winter.

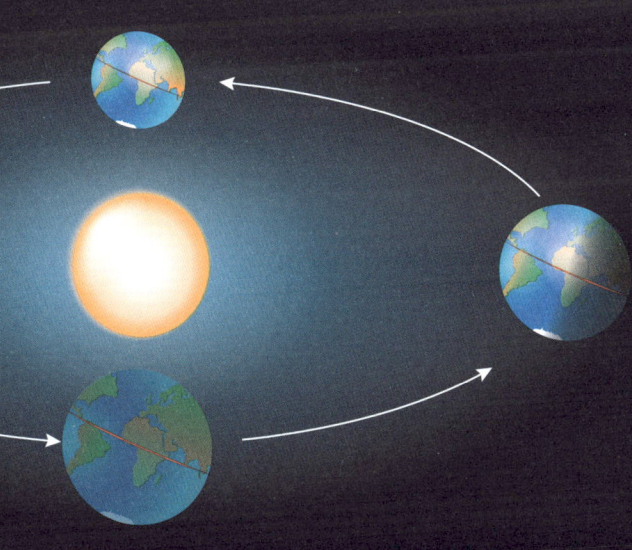

About the author

Have you always been an author?
No, but I've been writing for a long time, because I was a sports journalist on a newspaper for many years. Then when my youngest daughter was born, I made the move from writing articles about footballers to writing stories for children.

Simon Yeend

What do you like about writing?
I find it relaxing and mentally stimulating at the same time. The hardest part is when you're staring at a blank page and thinking, *What shall I write?* Then you put down a few words, add a few more and you're away! And, of course, the best bit is when you get the actual book in your hands, because that is the reward for all the hours you spent writing it.

Why did you want to write this book?
I love writing adventure stories, and I also love learning new facts. This book allowed me to do both. And I love creating characters like Zax, who I hope you enjoy reading about as much as I enjoyed writing about him.

Would you want to visit another planet?
Erm, no! I'll leave that to the astronauts. I got sick on a rollercoaster once, and leaving the Earth's atmosphere would be WAY bumpier than that!

Was it fun imagining what Zax might make of Earth?
Definitely! What I had to do was imagine that I was seeing Earth for the very first time. So, what would stand out? From space, Earth might look like a giant blueberry – that is going mouldy! And clouds look like something you could definitely eat – giant bits of candyfloss floating in the sky. And probably my favourite part of the story was imagining what Zax would think about humans and our behaviour. Like how he was shocked when Aisha sneezed and how he thought her face had exploded. A sneeze, when you think about it, is quite weird.

Did you have to do lots of research?
Yes! But it was really interesting and fun to do. And I learnt so much. For example, I knew Mars was called the Red Planet, but I didn't know why it was red. Also, that there is a crater on the Moon, that is so big, it would stretch from London to Moscow! And the crater was formed when a giant asteroid crashed into the Moon billions of years ago!

What's your favourite fact about planet Earth?
Here's a fact that didn't make it into the book, but I love it anyway. Did you know that you can see penguin poo in the Antarctic from space? Which is both gross and fascinating at the same time. Also, the fact that Earth is in EXACTLY the right spot in the solar system for life to exist on it. Not too hot. Not too cold. And with oxygen and water which are essential for life.

Do you think Zax will visit any other planets?
Definitely. He's a smart and inquisitive alien. He will travel far and wide. But he will also come back to see Earth and his new friends Aisha and Nathan.

About the illustrator

Do you illustrate digitally, or with pens and paints?

For professional work I prefer to work digitally since it allows me to be faster and cleaner. For personal work or fun I like to play around with traditional techniques.

Daniel Limon

How did you decide what the alien Zax should look like?

Zax's features were suggested by the author, an alien with red skin, purple teeth, and four arms. The rest, such as proportions, expressions, and gestures, I created myself by imagining what the character would be like according to what he does and how he behaves in the story.

Do you prefer to illustrate fiction, or non-fiction books?

Wow, good question! I love both! In fiction it's pure imagination, but I have a very curious nature and I enjoy learning things which non-fiction books allow me to. I especially enjoy learning about science and history.

What did you like best about illustrating this book?

I liked everything, but especially illustrating the scenes on Mars, the Moon, and the scenes of space in general.

What was the most challenging thing about illustrating this book?

The first big challenge was creating the characters, the second and greatest challenge was the schedule. This time, we would have needed a time-machine from another planet to get the work done at a relaxed pace!

Do you base human characters on people you know?

Yes, I always think about my children and nieces and nephews when creating characters, depending on their age. For example, I ask myself what did Marina and Alex look like when they were eight years old?

Which was your favourite scene to draw in the book?

Definitely the scene where Nathan presses the wrong button and panic breaks out, I find it really funny. I also really liked the meteorite and Mars scenes.

Do you think there might be aliens somewhere out there in the universe?

For sure! And I hope they all look like Zax!

If it were possible, would you like to visit another planet?

I would like to, but I think we live on the best planet there could be. So the important thing is for us all to take care of it and leave the rest of the planets for literature and science fiction.

Book chat

What did you think this book would be about? Were you right?

What was fun about learning about Earth from Zax?

Has this book made you look at anything differently?

What is your favourite fact from the book?

Did any parts of the book make you laugh?

If you were an alien visiting Earth, what do you think you'd find strange?

Would you like to visit another planet? Why or why not?

If you could ask Zax anything, what would you ask?

Book challenge:

Imagine you have landed on Zax's planet, Glibberon. Draw what you can see.

Published by Collins
An imprint of HarperCollins*Publishers*

The News Building
1 London Bridge Street
London
SE1 9GF
UK

Macken House
39/40 Mayor Street Upper
Dublin 1
D01 C9W8
Ireland

Text © Simon Yeend 2025
Design and illustrations © HarperCollins*Publishers* Limited 2025

Simon Yeend asserts his moral right to be identified as the author of this work.

10 9 8 7 6 5 4 3 2 1

ISBN 978-0-00-876782-2

All rights reserved. No part of this publication may be reproduced, stored in a retrieval system, or transmitted in any form by any means, electronic, mechanical, photocopying, recording or otherwise, without the prior written permission of the Publisher or a licence permitting restricted copying in the United Kingdom issued by the Copyright Licensing Agency Ltd, 5th Floor, Shackleton House, 4 Battle Bridge Lane, London SE1 2HX.

Without limiting the exclusive rights of any author, contributor or the publisher of this publication, any unauthorised use of this publication to train generative artificial intelligence (AI) technologies is expressly prohibited. HarperCollins also exercise their rights under Article 4(3) of the Digital Single Market Directive 2019/790 and expressly reserve this publication from the text and data mining exception.

British Library Cataloguing-in-Publication Data
A catalogue record for this publication is available from the British Library.

Download the teaching notes and word cards to accompany this book at:
http://littlewandle.org.uk/signupfluency/

Get the latest Collins Big Cat news at
collins.co.uk/collinsbigcat

Author: Simon Yeend
Illustrator: Daniel Limon (Beehive Illustration)
Publisher: Laura White
Commissioning editor and
 product manager: Caroline Green
Series editor: Charlotte Raby
Development editor: Catherine Baker
Project manager: Emily Hooton
Copyeditor: Sally Byford
Proofreader: Catherine Dakin
Cover designer: Sarah Finan
Typesetter: 2Hoots Publishing Services Ltd
Production controller: Sophie Waeland

Printed in the UK.

MIX
Paper | Supporting responsible forestry
FSC™ C007454

This book contains FSC™ certified paper and other controlled sources to ensure responsible forest management.

For more information visit: www.harpercollins.co.uk/green

Made with responsibly sourced paper and vegetable ink

Scan to see how we are reducing our environmental impact.

Acknowledgements
The publishers gratefully acknowledge the permission granted to reproduce the copyright material in this book. Every effort has been made to trace copyright holders and to obtain their permission for the use of copyright material. The publishers will gladly receive any information enabling them to rectify any error or omission at the first opportunity.

p10 NASA Goddard/NASA, p13 Vina amelia/Shutterstock, p14t singh srilom/Shutterstock, p14b Airpano/Amazing Aerial Agency/Science Photo Library, p15t Eleseus/Shutterstock, p15b takayuki/Shutterstock, p16 Panga Media/Shutterstock, p22 Dmitry Pichugin/Shutterstock, p23t Annamarita Sofis/Shutterstock, p23b Jhampier Giron M/Shutterstock, p38t Dan Kosmayer/Shutterstock, p38b SweetLeMontea/Shutterstock, p39 chert28/Shutterstock, p45 NASA Goddard/NASA, p54 JPL-Caltech/ESA/NASA, p55t Solar Dynamics Observatory/GSFC/NASA, p55b Harvepino/Shutterstock, p56 JPL/NASA, p59 Science Photo Library/Alamy, p63 NASA/Science Photo Library, p66 JPL-Caltech/SwRI/MSSS/NASA, p72 NASA Goddard/NASA, p76 James Thew/Alamy, p86 JPL-Caltech/UCLA/MPS/DLR/IDA/NASA, p87 ESA/ATG medialab/NASA, p100 Roman3dArt/Shutterstock, p105 Designua/Shutterstock.